Peaceful like a Panda

For all the parents, caregivers, and teachers
doing the incredibly important work of teaching
mindfulness to our next generation −K.W.

For Kamal, Emmett, and Sabrina −A.B.

Text copyright © 2020 by Kira Willey
Jacket art and interior illustrations copyright © 2020 by Anni Betts

All rights reserved. Published in the United States by Rodale Kids, an imprint of Random House Children's Books, a division of Penguin Random House LLC, New York.

Rodale and the colophon are registered trademarks and Rodale Kids is a trademark of Penguin Random House LLC.

Visit us on the Web! rhcbooks.com

Educators and librarians, for a variety of teaching tools, visit us at RHTeachersLibrarians.com

Library of Congress Cataloging-in-Publication Data is available upon request.
ISBN 978-0-593-17924-6 (hardcover) − ISBN 978-0-593-17926-0 (trade pbk.) −
ISBN 978-0-593-17925-3 (ebook)

The artist created the illustrations for this book digitally.
The text of this book is set in 14-point Intro.
Interior design by Jan Gerardi

MANUFACTURED IN CHINA
10 9 8 7 6 5 4 3 2 1
First American Edition

Peaceful
like a Panda

30 Mindful Moments
for Playtime, Mealtime,
Bedtime—or Anytime!

Kira Willey

Illustrated by Anni Betts

Rodale Kids RODALE KiDS New York

Contents

Introduction • vi

1
Rise and Shine

15
Are We There Yet?

29
Brain Boosters

43
Playtime

57
Let's Eat

71
Good Night

Conclusion • 85

Introduction

Are you looking for a meaningful way to connect with your child, one that will help you feel fully present? Does your child need to learn how to release tension and stress? If you're a teacher, do your students struggle with anxiety or have a hard time focusing?

Mindfulness—simply defined as paying attention to the present moment with kindness and curiosity—has been proven effective at helping with all these things and more (including promoting better sleep, boosting the immune system, and alleviating symptoms of depression).

But how do we practice it with our children, especially if we're not trained?

You have all you need, right in your hands.

There are three key elements to practicing mindfulness with kids: keeping it short, fun, and consistent. *Peaceful Like a Panda* was written with this in mind. As in my first book, *Breathe Like a Bear,* the exercises here are concise; each takes about a minute to do. And as in that book—also beautifully illustrated by Anni Betts—the concepts are playful so they'll capture the imaginations of young children.

I've made the consistency part a no-brainer—each chapter is divided into times of day, so it's incredibly easy to fit an exercise (or two or three) into even the busiest of days. You can build mindfulness into your daily routine by attaching it to something you do regularly, like traveling to school, eating together, or reading a story at bedtime.

There are lots of fun choices. Start the day on a calm, sunny note with "Sun Breath," or get energized with "Wake-Up Wiggle." Give your brainpower a boost with "Owl Breath," and get some of those sillies out during playtime with "Ha-Ha Hyena!"

The whole family can practice mindful eating together with "Where's It From?"—considering the journey your food made to get to your plate. And when it's time for bed, help your child let go of all their troubles with "Good Night, Worries," setting the tone for a peaceful night's sleep.

Mindfulness is also an incredible vehicle for teaching social-emotional skills, and the exercises in this book are designed to help children develop self-awareness, practice optimism and gratitude, improve self-esteem, and make positive choices.

Imagine a generation of children who grow up with the skills to cope with stress and anxiety, who are able to thoughtfully respond to tough situations, and who have the self-awareness to manage their emotions and behavior. What a game changer for the future.

That's what you can help create, starting right now.

And the bonus? When you practice these exercises with your child, you get all these benefits too!

I'd love to hear from you. Please get in touch! You can find me at kirawilley.com.

Wake-Up Wiggle * 4

Sun Breath * 6

Good Morning, Body! * 9

How's the Weather? * 10

Word of the Day * 12

Do you ever have a hard time getting going in the morning? These fun, easy exercises can help—they're perfect to do as soon as you get up, after breakfast, or on the way to school. Pick your favorite one, and do it every morning. It'll help you get off to a good start— and then you're sure to have a GREAT day!

Wake-Up Wiggle

Are you sleepy?

Let's yawn a BIG yawn.

Now, even though you feel tired . . .
can you wiggle one toe? Just one?

Now wiggle another toe.

Keep those toes wiggling. . . .

And wiggle one finger. Just one!

Wiggle another finger.

Now wiggle your arms . . .
AND your legs . . .
AND your middle!

Wiggle your WHOLE body!

Keep going!

WIGGLE WIGGLE WIGGLE!

Now slow it down,
slow it down,
and hold still.

Sun Breath

Imagine you're the sun.

Take a big breath in, and as you let it out, send out your rays of sunshine.

Do it again. Take a big breath in, and as you let it out, send out your rays of sunshine.

Send them out in front of you . . . and out behind you.

Send them out to the left . . . and out to the right.

Send sunshine out in a big circle all around you.

You're spreading sunshine everywhere!

Feel it getting brighter and warmer all around you, every time you breathe in and out.

Time for a sunny day!

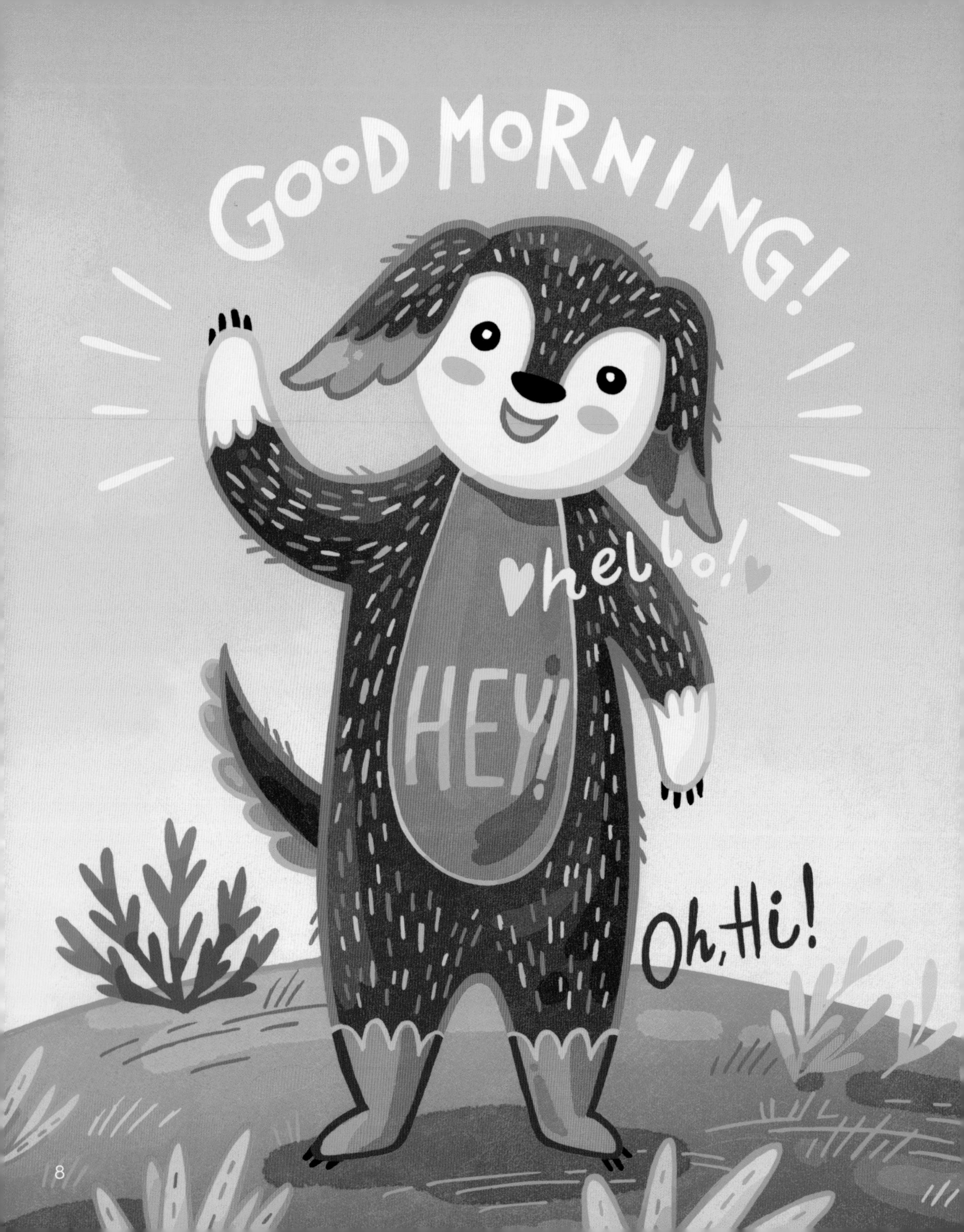
GOOD MORNING!
hello!
HEY!
Oh, Hi!

Good Morning, Body!

Let's say good morning
to our bodies.

Reach all the way down,
and tickle your toes.

Good morning, toes!

Now find your knees.

Oh, hi, knees!

Put your hands on your belly,
and give it a little rub.

Take a breath in, and let it out.

Hey, belly!

Put your hands over
your heart.

Take a breath in, and let it out.

Hello, heart!

Put your hands on your head,
where your smart brain is.

Take a breath in, and let it out.

Good morning, brain!

Bring your hands down.

Give your whole body a
little shake, and hold still.

Take a long breath in, and
let the air all the way out.

Good morning, body!

How's the Weather?

Maybe it's rainy outside today,
or maybe it's sunny.

What's the weather like inside you?

Take a long breath in, and let it
all the way out.

Do you feel bright and sunny today?

Do you feel gray and cloudy?

Or do you feel like something else?

Maybe it feels like a
thunderstorm inside you.

Or maybe it's a clear day.

Think about what kind of
weather it feels like inside
your body.

Any kind of weather is okay.

The weather is always
changing.

It will probably feel like
something different
tomorrow!

Take a long breath in,
and let it all the way out.

Word of the Day

Sit up tall. Take a big breath in, and let it all the way out.

Think about the day ahead of you.

How would you like it to go?

Pick a good word to finish this sentence:
"Today is going to be . . ."

You could pick a word like "amazing," "fun," or "awesome"!

Pick your own really good word.

If you'd like, tell your word to a grownup.

Try to remember your word all day!

Take a big breath in, and let it all the way out.

Red Light, Green Light * 18

Outside Inside * 20

Hot-Air Balloon * 22

Chugga-Chugga Train * 24

Heart Breath * 26

*S*itting in the car, on the bus, or on the train is the perfect time to practice simple mindfulness. Sometimes traveling is stressful, and these exercises can help you feel relaxed and calm. You might even see the world in a whole new way!

Red Light, Green Light

Hop into your car, and hold on
to the steering wheel.

Green light! Go!

Drive your car fast!

Red light! STOP.

Breathe in, and breathe out.

Breathe in, and breathe out.

Green light! Go!

Drive fast!

Red light! STOP.

Breathe in, and breathe out.

Breathe in, and breathe out.

Yellow light! Drive slooowly.

How slowly can you drive?

Red light! STOP.

Breathe in, and breathe out.

Breathe in, and breathe out.

Outside Inside

Hold your body still.

Take a breath in, and let it out.

Close your eyes if you want to.

Listen to the sounds outside.

What do you hear?

Do you hear people around you?

Do you hear music playing, an engine humming,
or the wind whistling by?

Listen.

Take a breath in, and let it out.

Now listen to the sounds inside.

What do you hear?

Is your belly making any noises?

Can you hear the sound of your breathing,
or your heart softly beating?

Listen.

Take a breath in, and let it all the way out.

Hot-Air Balloon

Let's go on a hot-air balloon ride!

You can take your balloon anywhere you want.

Take quick, short breaths in through your nose: sniff, sniff, sniff, sniff, sniff.

As you breathe in, lift your arms out to the sides and up toward the sky.

You're filling up your balloon with air so it can fly.

Breathe out slowly. Bring your arms back down.

Do it again!

Take short, quick breaths in through your nose: sniff, sniff, sniff, sniff, sniff.

Lift your arms out and up.

Breathe out. Bring your arms back down.

Do it again, as many times as you want.

It's time for an adventure!

Chugga-Chugga Train

Let's get our train moving down the tracks!

We'll start slowly.

Breathe in, and slowly say "Chuuugga Chuuugga Choooooo. . . ."

FAST TRAIN!

Breathe in.

Super fast, say "CHUGGA CHUGGA CHUGGA CHUGGA CHUGGA CHUGGA CHOO!"

Slow train.

Breathe in. Slowly say "Chuuugga Chuuugga Choooooo. . . ."

FAST TRAIN!

Breathe in! "CHUGGA CHUGGA
CHUGGA CHUGGA
CHUGGA CHUGGA CHOO!"

Reeeally slow train. Breathe in.

"C h u u u g g a C h u u u g g a
C h o o o o o o ..."

Time for our train to STOP.

Hold very still.

Breathe in, and breathe out.

Heart Breath

Sometimes things can feel kind of crazy.

Especially when you have to go to lots of different places.

Maybe you have to be in the car, on the bus, or on the train.

That's a lot!

Even when it's busy around you, you can take a little rest.

Put both hands over your heart.

Close your eyes, or look down toward your lap.

Take a long breath in, and let it all the way out.

Say "I can rest."

Take a long breath in, and let it all the way out.

"I can rest."

Take a long breath in, and let it all the way out.

"I can rest."

BRAIN BOOSTERS

Flamingo * 32

Puppy Shake * 35

I Am Smart! * 37

Owl Breath * 38

Starfish * 40

Did you know mindfulness can help you learn? The exercises in this chapter are like brain food—they'll make it easier for you to focus on what you need to do. Take a quick break to practice these activities anytime you feel like your brain is getting a little mushy. You'll be back on track in no time!

Flamingo

Stand up tall, with your feet flat on the floor.

Lift one knee up toward your belly.

Keep your belly strong!

If you feel wobbly, hold on to something or someone.

Spread your wings out wide to the sides.

You're a flamingo!

Breathe in, and breathe out.

Hold your body as still as you can.

Breathe in, and breathe out.

Slowly put your knee down.

Let's try it again!

Lift your other knee up toward your belly.

Keep your belly strong!

If you feel wobbly, hold on to something or someone.

Spread your wings out wide.

Hello, flamingo!

Breathe in, and breathe out.

Hold your body as still as you can.

Breathe in, and breathe out.

Slowly put your knee down.

Puppy Shake

Imagine you're a puppy,
and you just had a bath.

You're all wet!

Give your head and
shoulders a tiny little shake.

Give your arms a medium shake.

Give your legs a big shake.

Give your whole body a
HUGE shake!

Can you shake your tail?

Shake, shake, shake,
little puppy!

Shake, shake, shake!

Start to slow down.

Slow down a little more.

Hold your body still.

Breathe in, and breathe out.

SMART!

I Am Smart!

Take a long breath in, and let
the air all the way out.

Say "I am smart."

Breathe in, and breathe out.

Touch one hand to your head,
where your smart brain is.

Say it again: "I am smart!"

Breathe in, and breathe out.

Touch the other hand to your head,
where your smart brain is.

Give your head a little pat.

Say it again: "I AM SMART!"

Bring your hands down.

Take a long breath in, and let it
all the way out.

Owl Breath

Imagine you're an owl.

Sit up tall, and tuck your wings in to your sides.

Puff out your owl chest.

Open your eyes wide. Blink a few times.

Take a long breath in. Very softly, say "Hooo . . ."

Take another long breath in.

"Hooo . . ."

Blink your eyes a few times.

Take a long breath in. Really softly, say "Hooo . . ."

Once more, take a long breath in.

"Hooo . . ."

Gently shake out your wings.

Hold your body still.

starfish

Hold up one hand, and spread your fingers wide.

Pretend your hand is a starfish.

Can you trace the points of your starfish, all the way from your thumb to your pinkie?

With your other hand, slowly trace up the side of your starfish's first point. Breathe in.

Trace it down, and breathe out.

Trace up the next starfish point, and breathe in. Trace it down, and breathe out.

Keep going, nice and slow.

Trace up the next starfish point, and breathe in. Trace it down, and breathe out.

Trace up the next starfish point, and breathe in. Trace it down, and breathe out.

Now you're tracing your pinkie. . . .

Trace up the last starfish point, and breathe in. Trace it down, and breathe out.

Aaaahhh . . .

Ha-Ha Hyena! * 46

Let's Go Swimming * 48

Peaceful Like a Panda * 50

Butterfly Breath * 52

Hush, Baby * 55

Yahoo—it's time to play! Move, breathe, and get a little silly with these simple, fun mindfulness exercises that are great for building a healthy body and a healthy brain.

Ha-Ha Hyena!

Imagine you're a hyena in the jungle.

Hyenas love to laugh!

Put your hands on your belly.

Take a breath in.

Start with a baby laugh: "Ha ha ha."

Take a breath in.

Laugh a little more: "Ha ha ha ha ha!"

Take a looong breath in.

"HA HA HA HA HA HA!"

Take a really looong breath in!

"HA HA HA HA HA HA!"

What's so funny, hyena?

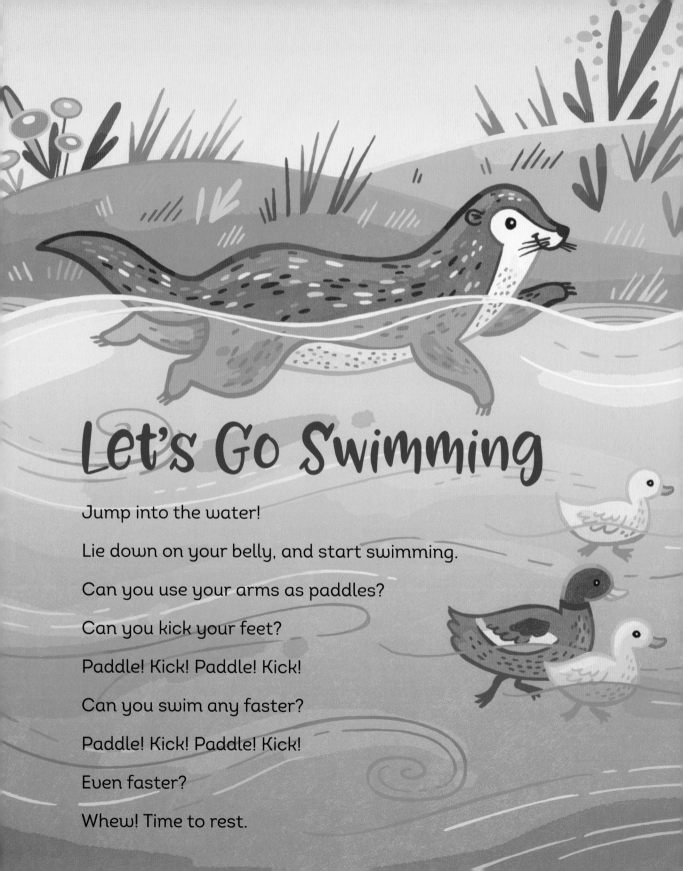

Let's Go Swimming

Jump into the water!

Lie down on your belly, and start swimming.

Can you use your arms as paddles?

Can you kick your feet?

Paddle! Kick! Paddle! Kick!

Can you swim any faster?

Paddle! Kick! Paddle! Kick!

Even faster?

Whew! Time to rest.

Lie on your back.

Take a long breath in, and let it all the way out.

Relax your whole body.

Float on the water.

Take a long breath in, and let it all the way out.

Float on the water.

Aaaahhh . . .

49

Peaceful Like a Panda

Pretend you're a big, furry panda bear.

Pandas love to eat, and they love to sleep.

Their favorite snack is bamboo.

Grab some bamboo, and take a bite.

Mmmm. Yum!

Rub your big, furry belly.

Breathe in, and breathe out.

Breathe in, and breathe out.

That was a good snack!

Time for a nap, panda.

Find a cozy spot, and
curl up in a ball.

Breathe in, and breathe out.

Breathe in, and breathe out.

Stay here as long as you like.

Butterfly Breath

Imagine you're a colorful butterfly.

Sit with the bottoms of your feet together
and your knees out wide.

Your knees are your butterfly wings.

Gently flap your wings up and down,
up and down.

Breathe in, butterfly.

Breathe out, butterfly.

What color are you?

Are you **purple** or *pink*, orange or **red**?

Gently flap your wings up and down, up and down.

Breathe in, butterfly.

Breathe out, butterfly.

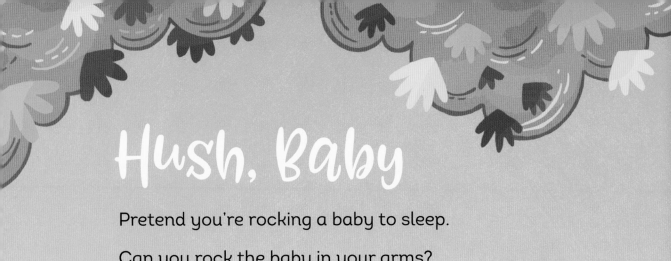

Hush, Baby

Pretend you're rocking a baby to sleep.

Can you rock the baby in your arms?

Rock your baby.

Side to side, side to side.

Take a long breath in, and whisper "Shhhhh . . ."

Take another long breath in.

"Shhhhh . . ."

Make the "shh" sound last as long as you can.

Is it working?

Try once more.

Take a long breath in, and whisper "Shhhhh . . ."

Softly!

Baby's sleeping!

Where's It From? * 60

Straw Breath * 63

See, Smell, Taste * 64

Thanks for the Food * 66

Ask Your Belly * 68

Raise your hand if you eat your food really fast! Yes, we all do sometimes. But it's not the best thing for our bellies. When we take a moment to slow down and think about our food and where it came from, we feel better and have more fun eating. Pick one exercise from this chapter and give it a try. And if you like it, go back for seconds!

Where's It From?

Look at the food in front of you.

Wait, don't have a bite yet!

Take a big breath in, and let it out.

Think about where your food
came from.

Did you buy it at a store?

How did it get there?

Maybe it came from a farm.

Or maybe it grew in a field.

Who grew it on the farm?

Who planted it in the field?

Think about the trip your
food took to get to you.

Think about all the people
who helped along the way.

Take a big breath in, and
let it out.

Time to eat!

Straw Breath

Sometimes we all feel a little overwhelmed.

Straw breath can help us COOL DOWN.

Imagine you're drinking through a straw.

Make the shape of a little "o" with your mouth.

Take a looong sip of air.

Relax your mouth, and let all the air out.

Haaaaaa . . .

Do it again!

Take a looong sip of air through your straw.

Relax your mouth, and let all the air out.

Haaaaaa . . .

Do it as many times as you like.

Try straw breath whenever you need
to cool down.

See, Smell, Taste

Look at your plate.

What colors do you see?

Is your food orange or red? White or green?

Say it out loud.

Now take a sniff.

What do you smell?

Does it smell spicy or sweet?

Or like something else?

Say it out loud.

Now take one tiny bite.

What does it taste like?

Is it warm or cold?

Say it out loud.

Eat up!

Thanks for the Food

Take a long breath in, and let it all the way out.

Someone grew the food you're eating today.

Say thank you to the person who grew it.

Someone put your food in a package.

Say thank you to the person who put it in a package.

Someone served you that food.

Say thank you to the person who served it to you.

Take a long breath in, and let it all the way out.

Ask Your Belly

Should you eat a few
more bites?

Or are you full?

Well, ask your belly!

Take a breath in, and
let it out.

Close your eyes if it helps.

Put one hand on your belly.

Say "Belly, how do you feel?"

Pay attention.

You might need to
ask again.

Say "Hey, belly, how
do you feel?"

Pay attention.

Do you feel full?

Or do you need to
eat a little bit more?

Breathe in, and
breathe out.

You know what to do!

Belly, HOW DO YOU feel?

Good night

The Light in Me * 74

Jellyfish Breath * 76

Sleepy Mouse * 78

Give Yourself a Hug * 80

Good Night, Worries * 83

Getting lots of good rest is one of the most important things we can do to stay healthy. It's good for our bodies and our brains. But sometimes we need a little help settling down, and that's where these exercises come in. They'll help your body and your mind feel calm and peaceful. Pick one or two you like best, do them every night—and ask a grownup to join you. Sleep tight!

The Light in Me

Pretend there's a light inside you.

It's right in the middle of your belly.

The light is warm and glowing,
like a candle.

Imagine the light slowly getting
bigger and bigger.

It's shining down your legs and
out the tips of your toes.

It's getting even bigger. . . .

It's shining brightly in your chest
and filling up your heart.

It's shining down your arms and
out your fingertips!

It's shining up, up, up inside your body,
right out the top of your head!

The light is all around you.

Everything is warm and bright.

Jellyfish Breath

Let's do jellyfish breath.

Jellyfish like to float up and down on the ocean waves.

Lie down in a cozy spot, and put one hand on your belly.

Imagine your hand is a jellyfish and your belly is the ocean.

Close your eyes if you'd like.

Feel the waves go up and down as you breathe in and out.

Take a SLOW, BIG breath in,
and feel your jellyfish float up.

Let the air all the way out,
and feel your jellyfish float down.

Try it again.

Take a SLOW, BIG breath in,
and feel your jellyfish float up.

Let the air all the way out,
and feel your jellyfish float down.

Up, down.

Up, down.

Floating on the ocean waves.

Sleepy Mouse

Sit on your heels, and put your
head down on the floor.

Curl your body up in a little ball.

Just like a tiny mouse.

Breathe in, and breathe out.

Slowly . . .

breathe in, and breathe out.

Even more slowly . . .

breathe in, and breathe out.

Relax your whole body.

Such a sleepy little mouse you are!

Stay here as long as you want.

Give Yourself a Hug

Sit up tall, and stretch your arms out wide to the sides.

Take a big breath in.

As you let it out, wrap both arms around your body.

Squeeze your arms tight, and give yourself a big hug!

Wiggle side to side.

Thank you, body! You've done a lot today.

Let go.

Sit up tall again, and stretch your arms out even wider to the sides.

Take a big breath in.

As you let it out, wrap both arms around your body.

Squeeze them really tight!

Give yourself a big hug!

Wiggle side to side.

Thank you, body! You've worked hard today.

Let go.

Take a big breath in, and let it all the way out.

Good Night, Worries

Imagine you have a
little box in your hand.

It will hold all your worries
so you can have a good rest.

Do you have a worry?

Say it out loud.

Then put it into the box.

Do you have another worry?

Say it out loud.

Then put it into the box.

Say all your worries out loud.

They can be big worries, or
they can be small worries.

Put them all into the box.

Now put the top on tight!

Put the box somewhere
safe, or have a grownup
hold it for you.

You don't have to think
about those worries now.

You can rest.

Good night!

Conclusion

Mindfulness can help us calm down, focus our energy, and get rid of stress—but we have to practice it. So pick an exercise (or two) that works for you, and do it every day. It will help you and your family feel calm and peaceful. Just like a panda!

Thank You

To my super-smart and always-positive editor, Dani Valladares, for the million phone calls and all the guidance as the book took shape, and to Mallory Loehr for shepherding it through to completion.

To Anni Betts, whose incredible drawings bring the ideas alive in a vibrant and playful way.

To my agent, Susie Cohen, who never misses a trick!

Huge gratitude to the rest of the team at Penguin Random House: Jan Gerardi, Julie Gayle, Tara Grieco, Lili Feinberg, Bess Schelper Sampson, and Jenny Golub.

Thanks to my Right-Hand Person, Katie, for all she does (and she does a LOT). I have no idea how I functioned before she joined me.

Thanks so much to my family—David, Lola, Tristan, and Brody—for their support, feedback, and encouragement all along.

And finally, thank you to all the parents and teachers who bought *Breathe Like a Bear* and used it in their homes, classrooms, therapy sessions, and circle times, and who let us know how useful and important it was for you and your children. Your emails, reviews, and feedback helped us develop this book!

About the Author and Illustrator

Hilary Murphy Photography

Kira Willey is an award-winning children's music artist, kids' yoga and mindfulness expert, speaker, and creator of Rockin' Yoga school programs. She brings music, movement, and mindfulness to children through her books, performances, and albums, which have won Parents' Choice Gold and Independent Music Awards.

Anni Betts is a professional illustrator who creates vibrant, cheerful drawings for books, magazines, advertisements, greeting cards, and more. Originally from Illinois, she now lives in England with her family.